Nelson Mandela
Father of Freedom

Hakim Adi

HODDER
Wayland

an imprint of Hodder Children's Books

© 2000 White-Thomson Publishing Ltd

Produced for Hodder Wayland by
White-Thomson Publishing Ltd
2/3 St Andrew's Place, Lewes, BN7 1UP

Editor: Liz Gogerly
Cover Design: Jan Sterling
Inside Design: Joyce Chester
Picture Research: Shelley Noronha – Glass Onion Pictures
Proofreader: Alison Cooper

Cover: Nelson Mandela in 1996.
Title page: Nelson Mandela in Ciskei, South Africa in 1994.

Published in Great Britain by Hodder Wayland,
an imprint of Hodder Children's Books

The right of Hakim Adi to be identified as the author of this
Work has been asserted by him in accordance with the
Copyright, Designs and Patents Act 1988

A Catalogue record for this book is available from the
British Library

ISBN 0 7502 2818 0

Printed and bound in Italy by G. Canale & C.S.p.A.

Hodder Children's Books
A division of Hodder Headline Limited
338 Euston Road, London, NW1 3BH

Picture Acknowledgements
The publisher would like to thank the following for their
kind permission to use these pictures:

AFP 12; Associated Press 30; Camera Press 10, 11;
Express Newspapers 32; Hodder Wayland Picture
Library/ 7, 20/ © Peter Magubane, Associated Press 22/
© Sam Nzima 36/ © John Frost Historical Newspapers
25 (left); Hulton Getty 28, 29; Impact/ Robin Laurance
6/ Jeremy Nicoll 38; Link © Greg English 4, 40, 41(top
and bottom)/ 25, 26/ Mayibuye Centre 8, 9, 13, 18, 21,
23, 25 (right) 31, 32, 34; Popperfoto © Guy Tillin
(title)/ 5, 16, 17, 19, 33, 35, 37, 42, 43, 44, 45; Rex
Features 14, 15/ © Sipa Press 27; Topham Picturepoint
(cover), 24, 39.

Contents

'That Long Road to Freedom...'

It was 4.30 in the morning of 11 February 1990. Nelson Mandela had got up early. On that day, after more than 10,000 days as a prisoner, he was going to be a free man. There were many things to do that morning, including saying final goodbyes and packing. He had been a prisoner for twenty-seven years but his personal belongings, mostly books, filled only a dozen boxes.

At nearly 4.00 that afternoon Nelson Mandela took his first steps as a free man. Crowds of people, including supporters, and television and newspaper journalists from around the world, waited for him. When he raised his fist, the crowd cheered. He had become a symbol of freedom for South Africans to millions of people throughout the world.

> *'Your tireless and heroic sacrifices have made it possible for me to be here today. I therefore place the remaining years of my life in your hands.'*
> Mandela's first speech to the people of South Africa, 11 February 1990.

Nelson Mandela and his wife Winnie give a victory salute as he walks to freedom in 1990.

Nelson Mandela voting in South Africa's first democratic election in April 1994.

Later that year, Mandela left South Africa for a world tour. In the United States he spoke to Congress and in London he joined thousands at a concert at Wembley. In 1991, he was elected president of the African National Congress (ANC) and, in 1993, was awarded the Nobel Peace Prize. Then, on 10 May 1994, Mandela became President of South Africa and the leader of the people he had helped to set free.

Mandela's Birth

Nelson Mandela was born in a tiny village in the Transkei region of South Africa on 18 July 1918. He was called Rolihlahla by his parents, a name which means 'troublemaker' in the Xhosa language. Later in life Mandela was sometimes called Madiba, the clan name he inherited at birth.

The Transkei where Mandela spent his childhood.

'**Then the country was ours, in our own name and right. We occupied the land, the forests, the rivers: we extracted the mineral wealth below the soil and all the riches of this beautiful country.**'
Mandela writing about South Africa before European conquest.

His father, Gadla Henry, was a chief of the Thembu people of South Africa who speak the Xhosa language. Although he could not read or write, Gadla Henry was an important man, an adviser to the Thembu kings. He had four wives and thirteen children. His third wife, Nosekeni, was Mandela's mother. Mandela's childhood was filled with simple pleasures. He enjoyed swimming in the river or playing in the hills: 'Nature was our playground,' he recalled.

At that time South Africa was not ruled by Africans but by European settlers who had taken control of most of the land. When Mandela was still a baby, his father quarrelled with the local white magistrate and was sacked as a chief. He was no longer paid by the government and Mandela and his mother had to move to another village to be looked after by relatives.

Europeans took control of South Africa's wealth, opening diamond mines, such as the one shown in this old photo.

Early Life

When he was seven, Mandela became the first person in his family to go to school. For this big occasion, his father gave him his first pair of trousers. At school his teacher gave him the English name, Nelson – African names, he was told, were not to be used at school.

Two years later, Mandela's father died. He had to leave his mother and live in the royal palace with his guardian, Chief Jongintaba. As he grew up, Mandela liked to listen to the stories told by older people of the time before the Europeans came, when Africans ruled their own countries. Mandela found out how the Thembu had governed themselves. They had had their own parliament in which all men could speak.

The house where Mandela lived from the 1920s to 1939.

Mandela at the age of eighteen, in one of his earliest known photographs.

In 1934, aged sixteen, Mandela was sent to boarding school. Then, in 1939, he became a student at Fort Hare, one of the most famous university colleges in southern Africa, where African students from all over Africa came to learn.

Escape to Johannesburg

In 1940, when Mandela was twenty-two, his guardian had arranged a marriage for him. To escape marrying somebody he didn't love, Nelson ran away to Johannesburg – one of the largest cities in South Africa. Johannesburg was a growing city. People arrived every day from the countryside in search of work. Mandela met many people from all over South Africa.

Mandela first tried to find work in a gold mine, but soon decided he wanted to study to become a lawyer. Walter Sisulu, a businessman and local leader, became his close friend. He gave Mandela money to allow him to study part-time and helped him to find work at a law firm. The two men became lifelong friends and later would spend many years in prison together.

Johannesburg in the 1950s. The shops in the background were owned by Indians. Later they were pulled down to make this a 'white' area.

Witwatersrand University in the 1960s. As in Mandela's day, there were few African students.

The government and laws in South Africa discriminated against Africans and all those who were not Europeans. Mandela experienced racism at work and at the University of Witwatersrand where he was the only black student in the law department. But Mandela also met many people who were fighting against racism and trying to change South Africa.

'I discovered for the first time people of my own age firmly aligned with the liberation struggle, who were prepared, despite their relative privilege, to sacrifice themselves for the cause of the oppressed.'
Mandela speaking about his time at university.

Fighting for Justice

In Johannesburg, Walter Sisulu encouraged Nelson to attend meetings of the African National Congress (ANC). The ANC had been formed in 1912 to unite all Africans in the fight against discrimination and to take part in the running of their country. It had become the most important African organization in South Africa fighting against racism.

A gathering of ANC members in the early 1950s.

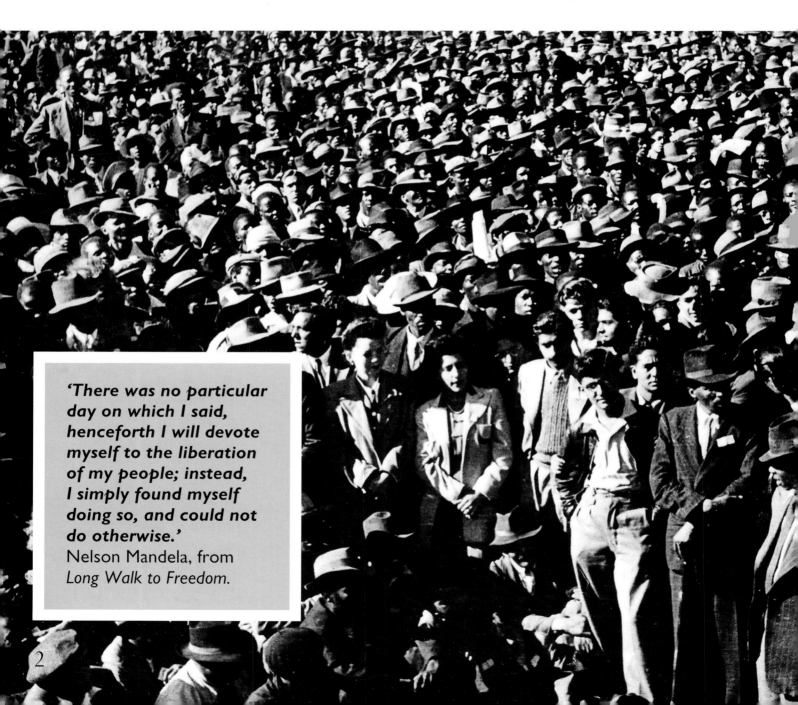

'There was no particular day on which I said, henceforth I will devote myself to the liberation of my people; instead, I simply found myself doing so, and could not do otherwise.'
Nelson Mandela, from *Long Walk to Freedom.*

In 1944, Nelson and other young men formed an ANC Youth League. They aimed to organize protests to force the white government to give Africans their rights. They were fighting for democracy and freedom for Africans.

Walter Sisulu's home became a meeting place where politics was discussed continually. Mandela even lived there for a short time and met his future wife, Evelyn Mase, who was studying to become a nurse. They were married in 1944, and a year later their first son, Thembi, was born. The following year, Evelyn gave birth to a daughter, Makaziwe, but the baby became ill and died nine months later.

Nelson with his first wife, Evelyn Mase.

13

Life under Apartheid

Only white people in South Africa were allowed to vote in government elections. In 1948, a new government was elected which introduced the policy of apartheid. Apartheid means 'separateness' in Afrikaans, the language of the first European settlers of Dutch origin. In South Africa, apartheid meant that the government passed laws to separate African, European and Indian people. These laws even stopped people of different backgrounds from marrying each other.

Africans, Europeans and Indians had to go to separate schools and live in separate areas. Under apartheid, Africans always had the poorest schools, hospitals and homes. In South Africa there were signs which said 'Europeans only' and 'Whites only' or 'Non-Europeans only' and 'Non-Whites only'. These signs were used in all public places, including beaches, cinemas and on public transport.

A sign points to a non-white eating house in Durban, South Africa in the 1950s.

Even before 1948, Africans had to carry a passbook showing that they had permission to be in a particular area. They were regularly stopped and checked by the police. Failing to produce the passbook could lead to arrest and imprisonment.

Apartheid stirs hatred and frustration among people. Young people, who should be in school or learning a trade, roam the streets, join gangs and wreak their revenge on the society that confronts them with only the dead-end alley of crime or poverty. Oliver Tambo of the ANC, writing in 1965.

In protest against apartheid, Nelson Mandela burns his passbook in March 1960.

Campaigning for Change

In 1950, Mandela became one of the leaders of the ANC. The ANC called for demonstrations, strikes and other protests against apartheid, even if this meant breaking the law. Mandela found that his busy political life often meant that he did not have the time to be at home with his family. His five-year-old son, Thembi, once asked, 'Where does Daddy live?'

In 1952, the ANC and other organizations launched the Defiance Campaign against the apartheid laws. They called for volunteers to break these laws, for example, by using toilets or other facilities reserved for white people. This action could force the government to change these unjust laws.

African and Indian men join together to resist the unjust laws.

FEMALE GAOL VROUE TRON

Female resisters in the Defiance Campaign being released from prison.

Mandela was appointed chief volunteer to lead the campaign. Thousands of people joined the campaign and many, including Mandela, were arrested. The government did not change the laws and actually introduced new laws to make protest more difficult. But the ANC had now taken action to achieve its goals and showed that its supporters were prepared to be imprisoned to achieve their freedom.

Independence

In 1952, Mandela started his own law firm. His partner was Oliver Tambo, his great friend who would later become the leader of the ANC. 'Mandela and Tambo' was the first black African law firm in South Africa. They were very popular with their African clients but still had to face racism in court.

That same year, Mandela was elected deputy president of the ANC and was one of many political leaders who were banned by the South African government. Banning people was a way of trying to stop protests against apartheid. It meant that Mandela could not attend any meetings. He could not even go to his son's birthday party.

Mandela with his lawyer partner, Oliver Tambo, in 1962.

The following year, Mandela was forced to resign from the ANC or face imprisonment and banning for another two years. These laws and other action by the government made Mandela realize that if Africans were to gain their freedom a new type of political struggle was needed.

Africans protest against apartheid.

The Freedom Charter

In 1954, the ANC decided to call a Congress of the People. This would be a meeting of representatives from all the people of South Africa. Together they would draw up a Freedom Charter. The Freedom Charter would set down in writing their plans for a future South Africa where all people would have equal rights, whatever their colour or background.

The People shall govern
All national groups shall have equal rights
The People shall share in the country's wealth
The Land shall be shared amongst those who work it.
Taken from the *Freedom Charter*.

Children hand out ANC leaflets in support of the Freedom Charter.

Leaflets were sent throughout the country asking people: If you could make the laws, what would you do? How would you set about making South Africa a happy place for all the people who live in it? Thousands of people sent in ideas and over 3,000 people attended the Congress in June 1955. The Congress was broken up by armed police but the people had produced their Freedom Charter. The Freedom Charter united all the organizations that were struggling to bring about a new South Africa. They became known as the Congress Alliance.

Throughout this time, Mandela lived under a ban. However, each night he took to the boxing ring. Training in the gym had become a welcome relief from the stress and strain of his political fight.

Mandela spars with boxing champion Jerry Moloi.

High Treason

In 1956, the South African government arrested all the leaders of the ANC and the Congress Alliance. Mandela and 155 others were charged with high treason. It was said that the Freedom Charter proved they were planning to violently overthrow the government. The court case lasted until 1961, when all the accused were declared innocent of the charges.

Unfortunately, Mandela's marriage to Evelyn broke up when he was in prison awaiting trial. She did not approve of his political work, and told him to choose between the ANC and their marriage.

Mandela (on the right) arrives at the Treason Trial in 1958.

In 1957, Mandela met Nomzamo Winifred Madikizela and, in 1958, they married. She became Mrs Winnie Mandela and joined the ANC. She took part in the protest against the pass laws, which restricted Africans' movements and forced them to carry passbooks. Eventually, she was arrested and was forced to spend two weeks in prison.

'The wife of a freedom fighter is often like a widow, even when her husband is not in prison.' Nelson Mandela speaking about Winnie Mandela.

Nelson and Winnie Mandela in 1958.

Sharpeville

Opposition to the unjust laws in South Africa continued to grow. Africans were inspired by other African countries that were becoming independent and were no longer ruled by Europeans.

In 1960, the Pan Africanist Congress (PAC), one of the other organizations fighting against apartheid, organized a campaign against the pass laws. In Sharpeville, near Johannesburg, a demonstration of thousands surrounded the police station. Although the demonstrators were unarmed, the police opened fire and killed almost seventy people, including women and children.

Rioting breaks out in Sharpeville following the shooting of unarmed demonstrators in 1960.

Daily Mirror TUES MAR. 22 1960
2½ No. 17,500

FURY IN SOUTH AFRICA

LIKE a battlefield. . . . Some of the 56 Africans killed and 162 wounded sprawled in a street after police had opened fire with rifles and sten guns at Sharpeville, near Johannesburg, South Africa, yesterday.
Women and children were among the victims.
Now turn to Back Page.

56 SHOT DEAD
162 WOUNDED

A report of the Sharpeville Massacre on the front page of a British newspaper.

'All told more than seven hundred shots had been fired into the crowd, wounding more than four hundred including women and children. It was a massacre and the next day press photos displayed the savagery on front pages throughout the world.'
Nelson Mandela writing about Sharpeville in *Long Walk to Freedom*.

Mandela in the early 1960s before his arrest.

The massacre at Sharpeville became headline news throughout the world. People everywhere saw how Africans were treated. Many governments and the United Nations protested to the South African government. Strikes and rioting grew more violent in South Africa.
In response, the South African government declared a State of Emergency and arrested Mandela and two thousand others. The ANC was declared an illegal organization which meant that its members could be arrested and imprisoned for up to ten years.

'The Black Pimpernel'

In 1961, the ANC leaders decided that they must carry on their struggle even though their organization was illegal. Mandela had to leave Winnie and their two young children, and go into hiding, where he could carry out his political activities secretly. In order not to be recognized he grew a beard, wore blue overalls and disguised himself as a chauffeur or gardener. He was now an outlaw but the police were unable to find and arrest him.

Mandela at a conference in Pietermaritzburg in March 1961, just before he went into hiding.

Mandela posed in traditional dress for this photo while he was in hiding in 1961.

During this time, Mandela suggested to the other ANC leaders that they might need to use violence to defeat apartheid. He argued that non-violence had not ended the unjust laws and, in any case, people were already defending themselves against the violence of the government. Finally, it was agreed to continue with the non-violent struggle, but also to create an army to fight against the government. This became known as Umkhonto we Sizwe, meaning 'Spear of the Nation', and Mandela became its first commander.

Travel Abroad

In 1962, Nelson secretly left South Africa to speak for the ANC at a conference of African countries and organizations in Ethiopia. This was the first time that he had travelled abroad. It was also an opportunity to visit many independent African countries, including Tanzania, Egypt, Ghana and Nigeria, and get support for the struggle for a new South Africa.

He met famous African leaders, including Julius Nyerere, the first president of Tanzania, and Sekou Toure of Guinea. He also met those Africans fighting for freedom in other countries such as Algeria and Mozambique.

Nelson Mandela in London in 1962.

28

> *'Poor people everywhere are more alike than they are different.'*
> Mandela talking about the poor in Ethiopia.

In Ghana he met his old friend, Oliver Tambo, who had been sent abroad to build up the ANC from outside South Africa. Mandela also travelled to London where he visited all the famous historical places he had read about, and met some of the UK's most important politicians.

Mandela finally returned to Ethiopia for two months' full military training. During his time there he saw that poor people in Ethiopia lived similar lives to those of black people in South Africa.

A street in Addis Ababa, the capital of Ethiopia, visited by Mandela in 1962.

The Rivonia Trial

A short time after his return to South Africa Mandela was arrested and charged with leaving the country illegally. He was tried, found guilty and sentenced to five years in prison. But while he was in prison, he was brought to court again with all the leaders of Umkhonto we Sizwe. They were charged with sabotage and attempting to overthrow the government.

The 1963 Rivonia Trial became the most famous in South African history. The government secretly recorded the conversations of the arrested men and even tortured some of them to try to get evidence. Mandela and the others expected to be executed if they were found guilty.

Winnie Mandela escorts Nelson Mandela's mother to court during the Rivonia trial.

Photos of the eight men sentenced to life imprisonment in the Rivonia trial. Nelson Mandela is on the top row, first left.

Demonstrators outside court during the trial.

Mandela decided that the best way to defend himself was to explain his beliefs, which he did for over four hours. He finished his speech with words that have since become famous (see box).

On Friday 12 June 1964, Mandela and seven others waited for the verdict. Winnie and Mandela's mother watched as they were found guilty. The only relief was that they did not face the death penalty. Instead they were sentenced to life imprisonment.

'During my lifetime I have dedicated myself to this struggle of the African people. I have fought against white domination and I have fought against black domination. I have cherished the ideal of a democratic and free society in which all persons live together in harmony and with equal opportunities. It is an ideal which I hope to live for and achieve. But if needs be it is an ideal for which I am prepared to die.' The conclusion of Mandela's speech at the Rivonia Trial, 12 June 1964.

31

Robben Island

At the age of forty-six, Mandela became a prisoner in one of the harshest prisons in the country, Robben Island. Robben Island was 29 kilometres off the coast of Cape Town, a long way from freedom. Mandela was cut off from news of his family and of the fight against apartheid.

Even in prison, laws discriminated against Africans. They were given the worst food and even made to wear short trousers. Mandela was forced to do hard labour, at first crushing stones to make gravel and later digging in a lime quarry.

Mandela sewing prison clothes before being sent to Robben Island.

The prison yard at Robben Island where inmates were made to crush stones.

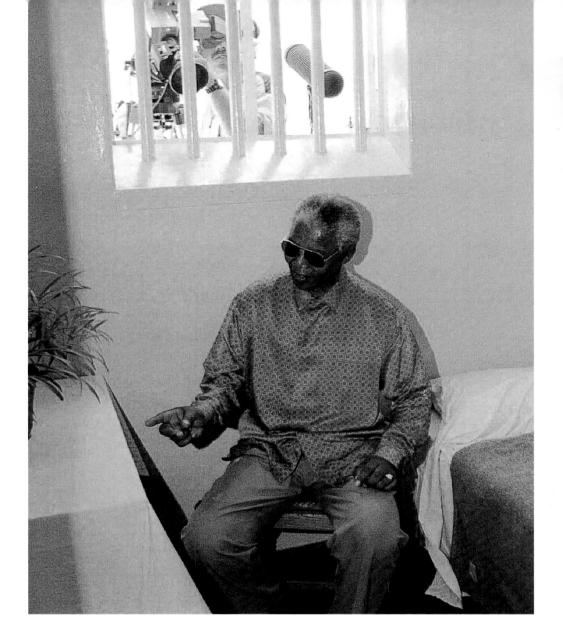

Mandela visits his old cell on Robben Island in 1995, on the fifth anniversary of his release from prison.

'We would fight inside as we had fought outside. The racism and repression were the same; I would simply have to fight on different terms.'
Mandela, *Long Walk to Freedom*.

Mandela's cell measured just 1.8 metres across. When he lay down, his head touched one wall and his feet the other. The walls were damp and each prisoner was given just three worn blankets and a straw mat on which to sleep. The cell had only one small window through which Mandela could see the courtyard below.

To survive the many difficult years, Mandela and his friends knew that they must support each other and continue to demand their rights to better conditions.

The World's Most Famous Prisoner

In twenty-seven years, Mandela saw some improvement in prison conditions. But there were punishments as well as privileges. When he was caught writing his autobiography he lost his right to study for four years.

For many years, Mandela was only allowed one visitor and one letter from his family every six months. The few letters he received were often impossible to read because they were censored. Visits were limited to thirty minutes and he was not allowed in the same room as his visitors. Prison warders listened to conversations between Mandela and his visitors in their separate rooms, and often interrupted them.

Mandela and Walter Sisulu photographed on Robben Island in 1964.

Mandela's daughter Zindzi campaigning for the release of her father and other political prisoners in 1985.

He was constantly concerned about the treatment of Winnie and his family. Winnie was sometimes banned or imprisoned for her political activities and was unable to visit for years at a time. Mandela was not allowed to see his daughter Zindzi for twelve years and unable to go to the funeral of his eldest son who was killed in a car accident.

From 1977 onwards, Mandela no longer had to do hard labour and spent more time studying for his law degree, teaching and learning from the younger prisoners. He also had more time for his hobbies which included reading and gardening.

'I do not recall a time when he showed any despondence, not even when Winnie was in jail, detained or when news came of her torture has Nelson flagged.' Mac Maharaj, another prisoner on Robben Island, talking about Nelson Mandela.

The Struggle Continues

While Mandela was in prison, the struggle against apartheid was continued by the workers, churches and especially the youth. Many young people were encouraged by the successful fight for independence in Zimbabwe, Angola and Mozambique, and by the new Black Consciousness movement in South Africa led by Steve Biko.

Friends carry away the body of Hector Peterson, the first victim at Soweto in June 1976.

In June 1976, thousands of African schoolchildren in Soweto protested against being taught in Afrikaans, the language of the government. During the demonstrations police opened fire and killed over 500 young protesters. Africans responded with many strikes and ANC attacks on police stations and other government buildings throughout South Africa.

'The thirst for freedom in children's hearts was such that they were prepared to face those machine guns with stones.' Winnie Mandela writing about the 1976 protests in Soweto.

Mandela and other political prisoners on Robben Island in 1977.

In 1983, 600 organizations formed the United Democratic Front to lead the fight against apartheid. By this time, the South African government had few friends in the world. In 1980, for example, the United Nations had called for the release of Mandela and other political prisoners. Many people supported the introduction of sanctions, forbidding trade and sporting links with South Africa.

In 1990, the government finally lifted the ban on the ANC and other organizations.

'Free Mandela!'

Demonstrators in London during 1984 demand free 'Nelson Mandela!'

Mandela had become the most famous prisoner in the world. Millions of people joined the anti-apartheid movements and the ANC campaign to 'Free Mandela!'

In 1982, Mandela was moved from Robben Island to Pollsmoor prison on the South African mainland. In Pollsmoor, Mandela lived in better conditions. He was also allowed in the same room as Winnie during visits. However, he missed the outdoor life of Robben Island and often felt lonely. In 1988, he was given his own house inside Victor Vorster prison. He was also allowed more contact with his friends and family.

Left **The struggle against apartheid was fought in many ways. Here an African sits on a seat reserved for whites only.**

Below **Many Africans gave their lives for freedom and democracy in South Africa.**

'**I cherish my own freedom, but I care even more for your freedom. I will not give any undertaking when you and I, the people, are not free.'**
Mandela's response to an offer of freedom from the South African government, read by his daughter Zindzi in a speech in 1985.

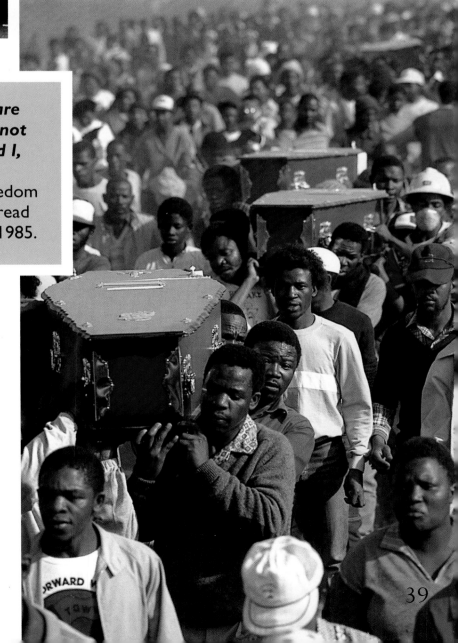

The South African government did make offers to free Mandela, but only if he would accept their conditions. This meant giving up the struggle against apartheid. Mandela refused. But, in 1986, he decided that he must begin talking to the government to prevent more violence in the country. So started the series of secret meetings which would lead to his freedom.

39

President Mandela

When Mandela was finally freed from prison in 1990, his freedom had become a symbol for the freedom of all South Africans. His refusal to accept racism and unjust laws, even if this meant spending years in prison, made him a hero. But it took the heroism of millions to force the South African government to end apartheid and, for the first time, allow all South Africans to vote in the election in April 1994.

South Africans queuing to vote in the country's first democratic election.

The ANC won the 1994 election and Mandela became the first black president of a democratic South Africa. Mandela wanted to encourage forgiveness and to unite all South Africans, so his government included African, Indian and white ministers — even though some had previously supported apartheid.

As the new president, Mandela found that it was often difficult to change South Africa quickly. Many Africans were still very poor, and sometimes there were violent protests in parts of the country. He also found that as president he still had little time to spend with his family. His marriage to Winnie ended in 1992.

Above **Nelson Mandela during the 1994 election campaign.**

'We shall build the society in which all South Africans, both black and white, will be able to walk tall, without any fear in their hearts, assured of their inalienable right to human dignity – a rainbow nation at peace with itself and the world.'
From Nelson Mandela's first speech as President.

Right **President Nelson Mandela with the former South African president F.W. de Klerk.**

South Africa's Ambassador

Even before he became president, Nelson Mandela had been invited to travel to many different foreign countries. A short time after his release from prison he toured throughout Africa, Europe, North America and Asia. In 1993, Mandela travelled to Oslo in Norway with the South African president, F.W. de Klerk. Both men had been awarded the Nobel Peace Prize for their efforts to bring about an end to apartheid and create a new democratic South Africa.

Mandela with F.W. de Klerk receiving the Nobel Peace Prize in 1993.

Nelson Mandela became his country's greatest ambassador and a symbol of the new South Africa. After he became president, he continued to pay visits to many other countries but also invited many of the world's most important political leaders to visit South Africa. Nelson Mandela tried to make sure that South Africa had good relations with many different countries. On a personal level, he was just as friendly with the communist Cuban leader, Fidel Castro, as he was with the president of the United States, Bill Clinton, and both leaders visited South Africa in 1998.

Mandela shows US President Bill Clinton his prison cell on Robben Island.

'South Africa's future foreign relations will be based on our belief that human rights should be the core of international relations, and we are ready to play a role in fostering peace and prosperity in the world.'
Nelson Mandela interviewed in 1993.

Retirement

When he was in his seventies Mandela met Graca Machel, the widow of the former leader of Mozambique, Samora Machel. They became close friends, and, just before his eightieth birthday in 1998, they married. He now has a partner with whom he can share the rest of his life.

In 1999, after five years as president, Mandela retired and returned to make his home in the Transkei where he had been born. In his retirement, he still finds time to travel throughout the world, but he has time to spend with his new wife and his family. He can finally do all the things that he did not have the time or the opportunity to do as a freedom fighter, a prisoner or a president.

Nelson Mandela and his new wife Graca at his eightieth birthday party.

Nelson Mandela has become one of the most famous men in the world — a man whom prime ministers and presidents like to call their friend. His willingness to sacrifice his own freedom, and even his life, for his beliefs and the freedom of his people has made him one of the great heroes of the twentieth century.

'I have walked that long road to freedom. I have tried not to falter; I have made missteps along the way. But I have discovered the secret that after climbing a great hill, one only finds that there are many more hills to climb. I have taken a moment here to rest, to steal a view of the glorious vista that surrounds me, to look back on the distance I have come. But I can rest only for a moment, for with freedom come responsibilities, and I dare not linger, for my long walk has not ended.'
Nelson Mandela.

Nelson Mandela with the Spice Girls and Prince Charles in 1997.

45

Glossary

Apartheid The system of apartheid in South Africa meant the separation of African, European and Indian people.

autobiography A book that somebody writes telling the story of their own life.

banned Under apartheid, a banned person was not allowed to attend meetings, meet more than one person at a time, or have their speeches mentioned in newspapers or on television.

censored To censor something means to inspect it and remove what is unacceptable. The prison authorities in South Africa would cut out the parts of letters that they did not like.

guardian Somebody who takes the place of a child's parent.

liberation Freedom.

magistrate Usually a person who judges minor cases in a law court.

oppressed Ruled without justice or any rights – as most people in South Africa were under apartheid.

privilege A right or advantage that can be given or taken away.

sabotage Deliberately destroying machinery or equipment, usually in order to weaken an enemy.

sacrifice Giving up something in order to get something else.

sanctions Measures taken against a country by other countries to force a change of policy.

State of Emergency Extraordinary measures, such as arresting opponents or using the army, taken by a government in order to stay in power.

United Nations The organization which represents all the governments of the world.

Further Information

Books for Younger Readers

Life Stories, Nelson Mandela by Richard Killeen (Hodder Wayland)

Live Wire Real Lives: Nelson Mandela (Hodder and Stoughton Educational, 1998)

Nelson Mandela by Jayne Woodhouse (Heinemann, 1999)

Nelson Mandela: No Easy Walk to Freedom by Barry Denenberg (Scholastic)

Books for Older Readers/Sources

Long Walk to Freedom by Nelson Mandela (Abacus, 1997)

Mandela – The Authorised Biography by Anthony Sampson (Harper Collins, 1999)

Nelson Mandela – A Biography by Martin Meredith (Penguin, 1997)

Nelson Mandela – the Man and the Movement by Mary Benson (Penguin, 1994)

Date Chart

1918, 18 July Nelson Rolihlahla Mandela is born in Qunu, near Umtata, Transkei, South Africa.

1944 Mandela helps to found the African National Congress Youth League.

1944 Mandela marries his first wife Evelyn Mase (divorced in 1958).

1950, March Mandela joins ANC National Executive.

1952 Mandela is elected volunteer-in-chief for ANC Defiance Campaign.

1952 With Oliver Tambo, Mandela opens first black legal firm in South Africa.

1952 Mandela is elected President of the Transvaal branch of the ANC and the Youth League and Deputy President of the ANC.

1952, December Mandela receives first of many banning orders confining him to Johannesburg for six months.

1955 Mandela becomes one of the organizers of the Congress of the People and helps to draft the Freedom Charter.

1956, December Mandela is arrested and tried for High Treason (Treason Trial lasted until 1961).

1958 Mandela marries Nomzamo Winifred Madikizela.

1961, March Mandela begins secret political work.

1961, June Mandela becomes first commander of Umkhonto we Sizwe.

1962, January Mandela leaves South Africa secretly for six months to travel.

1962, August Mandela is arrested and later sentenced to six years' imprisonment.

1963, October Mandela is charged with sabotage at the famous Rivonia trial.

1964, June Mandela is sentenced to life imprisonment on Robben Island.

1979 Mandela is awarded the Nehru Prize for International Understanding.

1980, June UN Security Council demands Mandela's release from prison.

1980, December Mandela is awarded the freedom of the City of Glasgow.

1982, April Mandela is moved from Robben Island to Pollsmoor Prison.

1985 Mandela refuses offer of freedom in exchange for renouncing political violence.

1987 Mandela begins secret talks with the South African government.

1988 Mandela is given his own private bungalow in the grounds of Victor Vorster prison.

1990, 11 February Mandela is released from prison after 10,000 days.

1991 Mandela is elected President of the ANC.

1993 Mandela is awarded Nobel Peace Prize.

1994, 10 May Mandela becomes President of South Africa.

1998, July Mandela marries Graca Machel.

1999, June Mandela retires from public life.

Index

Page numbers in **bold** refer to pictures as well as text.